I0098210

HOW TO PLAY THE GAME OF LIFE

A Guide on Maneuvering Through Life's Challenges

ASHLEY RAE

ISBN: 978-0-692-61013-8

Contact the Publisher:

Ashleyrae817@gmail.com

Dedication

This book is dedicated to my two Grand-mothers one that I never had the pleasure of knowing Doris Rae Stephens and to the only Grandparent I have ever known Thelma Howard (Granny).

My Grandmother's (Doris Rae) life was cut short due to her passing away before the age of 40. Therefore I want to take advantage of opportunities that I have that she didn't have or, didn't get to achieve. I also think my Granny didn't get to live up to her full potential because she was always working in order to financially provide for her children and others.

I sure hope my Granny has told my Grandmother great things about me. May you both rest peacefully....

Table of Contents

~

Making yourself feel good

Knowing what you want!

Depression

Acknowledgments

Thank you to my Mommy (Angela Goines-Hartfield) and my Daddy (Curtis Ray Walker) for creating me. Mommy, thank you for the tough love, the straight-forward talks (even when I didn't want them), and reminding me that I'm still your baby when I have my emotional moments. I'm a better person because of those conversations. Daddy, thank you for always having my back and explaining to me when I'm wrong, and why I am wrong. Thank you also for cramming entrepreneurship in my head. Even though I rejected the idea a lot, I moved forward with my ideas and business because of you. I am not a quitter because of you. To my step -father William Hartfield Please continue to love my Mom unconditionally and keep supporting her on all levels of love and life. It is really appreciated. My Mother and Father used to drive me crazy as a teenager. Now I look back and appreciate them so much more. I grew up with people that had parents that didn't care about where they lived or what they did. I am forever grateful for my overbearing parents. Even if you were one of those people that didn't have parents, appreciate them anyway because you're probably a hard worker because of it.

To my big sister Amber Shadd-Patterson (My Phylicia Rashad) thank you for being there when I needed it the most. There is nothing greater than the bond between siblings. I truly appreciate you listening to my sorrows, regrets, joys, and my dirty little secrets. Love you.

To my Auntie Timika Keathley I don't know where to begin. (This woman furnished my first apartment when I was 19 years old. Everything from silverware to my living room furniture). I'll start with thank you for really stepping up and being everything I needed. You are truly my second Mom.

To my Auntie Ebony Powell You are one of the hardest working people I know. I love you. You do not have to be responsible for everyone.

Sheila Goines-Thank you for assisting me on my journey through college. I would not have been able to do it without you. I also appreciate all your good advice.

LaTonya Williams (B.A.)- You will always be my Auntie and I love you...

To my nieces Dayanna, Hunter, and Whitney (The Patterson children)! I LOVE YOU! Chase your dreams, learn everything you can, always listen to me, and never be afraid to talk to me. I will always guide you in the right direction no matter the situation without judgment. You will never have to worry about me repeating our discussions to anyone not even your parents. Dayanna follow your heart and keep your spirits high no matter the circumstance. Hunter, continue to become the resilient and excellent dancer that you are. Open up more and you'll be unstoppable. Remember that your life as a teenager is easy so enjoy and don't be afraid to try new things. To my brainchild Whitney. You remind me so much of myself as a little girl. Keep excelling and reaching new heights. Your entrepreneur spirit is sure to make Whitney incorporated a success.

Zetta and Jeanine; I think I am the closest to you both out of all of my cousins. Thank you for your guidance, advice, and leadership. We need another girl's trip.

To my cousins! Keep in mind I have about 35 first cousins so if your name is not mentioned it's just simply because I forgot but know that I love you all. Kareem, Jalen (Skylar), Peyton, Lexus, Brittany (Kassi Miiangel), Destiny, Destini, Jazmin, Donavon, Donald Goines III (R.I.H.), Blair (Chunky), Mariah, Jennifer, Trevon, Danyell, Candis, Christian, Angela, Asia, Sydney, Kaleb, Corey, and Denzel. Regardless if we talk or not my love for my blood never changes.

TO MY FAMILY

Uncle Mark, Uncle Tony (R.I.H.), Uncle Darren (Wood), Uncle Mooka (R.I.H.), Uncle Chris (Felt) Uncle Donald (Nudy), Uncle Michael (Deuce), and Uncle Thomas (Walker). I love you all and I appreciate everything you have ever done for me or with me. Shout out to my Howard and Cannon family! Also to my Powell family Victoria, Kwame, Robert (Chaka), Auntie Zetta (Rosie), and Gi Gi.

To my God-daughter Anaiah Campbell- Keep striving academically. I can certainly see you doing well at an Ivy League school. Don't be shy and always be willing to communicate. To my God son Khalil Taylor- I hope you grow to be a well rounded, loving, educated, and understanding young man.

THANK YOU FOR BEING A FRIEND.......

I always hear people talk about how they don't have friends. I can't help but hurt for them because that must be an awful feeling. I'm very grateful for mine.

Janell Taylor, LaGail Odoms, Mallory Sotherland, Ariel Jones, Ashley Campbell-Horne, Cierra Patrick, Sherese Bennett (Chance), Carla Simpson, Lorri Thomas, Katrina Hamilton, Miles Hamilton, Breon McCray, Chidiebere Nwosu, Darralyn Manning,

Keshia Maples, LaChae Culberson, Lauren Culberson, Tashema Adams, Aleasia Adams, Andronika Calloway, Annette Perry (R.I.H.), My mentor Aja Thornton, Ophelia Epps, Jazmine Williams, and Marcel Friday (Williams).

Introduction

This all started last year in December of 2014. My forever friend LaGail and I were making Vision boards for the New Year. We were talking about things that we want to accomplish or at least take steps toward certain accomplishments. She always tells me that I'm always looking on the brighter side of situations or trying to make things better with some sort of positive commentary. Which, I appreciate her saying because I really do like to try to make people feel better. She's made this comment a few times. I wrote down a few things that I wanted to do that I didn't add on my vision board and writing a book was one those things. Since LaGail kept talking about my glass half full thinking I decided to write a book that could possibly help people deal with everyday life problems.

I actually wrote out a title and a list of chapters, closed the notebook and didn't entertain the idea of writing a book again. A few months later my podcast partner told me that I should write a book. Luckily we were in front of one another getting ready to record and I just so happened to open the very same notebook that had my book chapters and titles written down. I got all excited and I said: "Look, I forgot I was supposed to write a book already here's the outline." She rolled her eyes at me because she always wants me to do more.

I think I was trying to pace myself because I had just started a blog called *LetsTalkRaeStyle.com* in March 2014. As I mentioned previously, my podcast partner and I have a podcast called Tenacious Talk. Not to mention that I have what we call a 9-5 and I also have a small business. Let's just say my plate is kind of full. I get nervous about my projects, which I think is understandable for any type of artist. Truthfully I have always thought about writing due to my uncle Donald Goines II (There are pretenders out here going by the same name I'm here to tell you if he doesn't know me he's a FRAUD) being a published Author and of course my deceased Grandfather Donald Goines being a published Author. Not to mention my Mother is a great non published writer and so is my Dad actually. So here I am.

I really hope that you enjoy this book and that you can apply some of what I have written into your life. I really did try to give examples of experiences from my own life, others around me, and stories that I have heard. There are so many books out here that try to assist people with life, but to me, or at least the ones that I have read didn't seem realistic. You don't need 200-300 pages of repetitive statements or long analogies that probably don't even apply or relate to you in anyway.

Chapter 1

Making yourself feel good

Every day in life we are faced with challenges. Not only do we have challenges but we also get involved in the challenges that our loved ones face as well. I know personally I provide advice to friends and family when asked and even when I am not asked. At times that can become a problem but my intentions are always good and for the best interest of my loved ones. However, there are always those few people that have more issues than you bargained for and by that I'm referring to the person or persons that cause and create their own drama.

How to Play the Game of Life

DRAMA

It's always something with them. They got into some sort of confrontation with their significant other. They call you asking for advice, which you don't mind providing but at the end of the conversation you realized that every word you said was a waste. It was a waste because they made every bad action against them excusable all in the name of LOVE so they say. You know there will be a next time. Next time it'll be a new significant other. People that place themselves in the exact position that they were previously in really aren't looking for help. They feed and thrive off the drama that they create. It's not hard to recognize but it's unfortunate because who wants to think of their friend as a Drama lover and I am not talking about theatre!? Then you start to realize that every relationship he or she has is treacherous. They have issues with everyone from their parents to their significant other. They function off of dysfunction.

Everyone has a friend or family member that is overly sensitive. Either they are mad because someone didn't invite them somewhere or he or she took a comment the wrong way. Everything makes them explode or cry. Maybe they do both, explode and then cry later. When they call you and start to tell you "what happened" you try to listen without interruption because you already know where this is headed. I usually interject when the words of the conversation begin to get too malicious. Right before they decide to let the bad take over the good in them I try to shift what they are viewing as hurtful behavior to a different angle. To a person that's overly sensitive they almost always feel as if someone is doing something to them on purpose. They are defensive! Always on guard! I often have to keep that in consideration when I'm attempting to give advice. Altering the angle of their view can change how they feel about the situation. Changing their view may actually help them understand themselves and people a little better in all other circumstances.

BLAME

Let's not forget the BLAMER. You know the person that blames everything on everyone else? They never take ownership for the events that have occurred in their lives? This kind of person typically likes to hold grudges and lack the gift of forgiveness as well. Whenever something happens (we know things always happen) they have a reason why it's not their fault even though the actions of this person directly affected the outcome. It's extremely hard having discussions with this kind of person because they have a combative response to anything you say. Please don't confuse this person with a realist, because they are totally different. The Blamer didn't lose their job because they were late every day. In their minds they lost their job because the boss can't stand them. They think that they've done everything right when in the real world they haven't because no one does everything right; especially not all the time. These people are constantly looking for someone to help them when really they just want someone to blame for not helping them. How I deal with this type of person is by asking them what they think they could have done to make the situation better, or to have a different outcome. Then I try to explain what I would have done in the same situation. Sometimes it helps and sometimes it doesn't, but people with this character trait are hard to sway especially when a troublesome situation first erupts.

PITY PARTY

There is always something wrong with this person. If you are the go to person for talks and advice you probably talk to this individual more than anyone else. It's not that they don't have a happy or normal life it's just that some people often get the short end of the stick or at least they think they get the short end of the stick. It seems that everything that happens to them is exaggerated. Yet, somehow you feel bad for them whenever you have discussions. Every time they suck you back into a sob story. You find yourself trying to figure out what you can do to make their lives better. I know I do! I'm always trying to figure out how I can help. What I can do? Even if I don't mention it to them, I'm thinking about it. Everything that happens is really not for everyone to know. Pity party people need the concerns, affections, and pity from other people it seems. It's kind of how they determine you care. All you can really do is show your support, which, is probably what you always do and hope you aren't completely drained of your energy. All of these situations/kinds of people can be draining at times. That's when you have to take a step back and ask yourself if you are okay. Are you okay with looking at yourself in the mirror? I am always trying to guide someone in the right direction when it comes to advice or just comfort. I noticed that I was burning myself out. I would become so disgruntled if someone didn't take the advice knowing that it was really what was best for them. I've actually had breakdowns when I found out one of the girls I mentored made some horrible decisions. I know that may sound extreme but it's very frustrating when you provide what many children and teens are lacking or looking for and, the person consciously makes poor choices. After all it is upsetting when you truly have a person's best interest at heart.

How to Play the Game of Life

NITPICKER

The nitpicker is the person that really isn't happy with themselves and has to rip other people apart in order to feel better about themselves. They will point negative things out about their friends or strangers. It really doesn't matter to them because they are unhappy. This person is also the person that continuously expresses how perfect their life is and how they are glad that they don't have the problems of other people. What they don't mention is what exactly their problems are! They don't tell you for a good reason. The reason is because they don't want to be picked apart by others even though that's what they do to people. I have no advice almost ever for these kinds of people, besides they are not nice, that's inappropriate, and when you point a finger there are three fingers pointing back at you (I know totally old school and cliché')! It's really just ugly behavior! I mean this isn't high school and we aren't the "Mean Girls."

The purpose of me providing examples of people that you may know is to show you how people pull from you on a regular basis. It's almost a routine. Sometimes we allow people to wear us out with their problems or concerns without considering our own. I'm not saying that you shouldn't comfort or console your friends. I am extremely guilty of making other people's problems my own. I'll be just as wound up or excited as them. The next thing you know I'm angry or sad or blaming someone else for something I'm responsible for. I call that behavior "emotional garbage dumping". Allowing everyone to throw their emotional garbage right off on me. I try to take on everything and then I'll end up neglecting myself.

I had to realize that ultimately I can only go so far on what I can absorb via conversation and how or what I can say as a response. Sometimes I don't respond I'll just sit and listen. What I'm saying is if being someone's support system interferes with your happiness then there is a problem. If you consult your friends or family and it always backfires on you then you have to reevaluate whom you choose to hold conversations with and whom you choose to support. When you end a conversation you shouldn't feel drained or empty. You shouldn't feel used or uncomfortable. We so often put the needs of others before our own and then wonder why we feel disconnected.

You have to do things that make you happy, even if that is not answering your phone or responding to a text message. Making your self feel good or happy is the beginning of self-satisfaction. You are responsible for yourself and your wellbeing. No one else can make you happy. You can't make anyone else happy without being happy. It sounds simple but it can be difficult depending upon the situation. Go places that bring you comfort and relaxation. Remind yourself that you come first! It's not being selfish or inconsiderate of others. We all need a break from people from time to time. It's totally normal. Mothers even need breaks from their children. Whatever you need to do to satisfy your basic need of happiness and regain peace of mind please get it accomplished.

Chapter 2

Knowing what you want!

When I graduated from high school I knew that my days in theatre class were over. I knew there was no more pretending and that I was being thrown into the real world. The real world requires money in order to eat and to have a place to live. I started my first semester of college at Wayne State University. I did not want to attend that school but my parents didn't want me to go away even if it were in the same state that we lived in which, is Michigan. Actually my Mother moved to Vegas right after I graduated from high school so, I have no idea why she was so adamant about me attending classes there. My sister attended Wayne State and so did my Aunt (Sheila). It was kind of inevitable. For the first time in my school life I was unsuccessful. I struggled in large classroom settings.

How to Play the Game of Life

To be perfectly honest it was super easy for me to drift into LA LA LAND or just to focus on something else. Now that I look back on that sector of my life I just wasn't ready. I remember a guidance school counselor asking me "why won't you just attend a community college first because it is so much cheaper" and, I just told her I didn't want to attend a community college. There was no real reason behind my answer.

In my second semester at Wayne State I made a deal with myself. If I didn't pass my Psychology class with a C at the very least I was going to transfer to Oakland Community College (O.C.C.) in January (which is when classes started back after Christmas break). I didn't tell anyone. That January I began studying at O.C.C. and I still consider that to be one of the best decisions I made in my life. I wanted to get my core classes over with so when I transferred back into a University I would only have to focus on my major. I did take some film classes at O.C.C. just to tap back into something that held my past interest. I attended O.C.C. all year around so that I would only be one year behind in college. Meaning I graduated in five years instead of four years. Thank God I didn't listen to any counselors because they advise you to take only 12 credit hours per semester. At that rate who knows when I would have graduated. I pumped out 16 to 17 credits my first semester there and then when summer classes rolled around I could take a lighter load. When I started at Oakland University (OU) I only had to take a total of 12 credits because I had taken so many at O.C.C... OU was an extremely different experience for me because I had never been surrounded by so many people that thought they knew everything when in all actuality they knew nothing about real life. Many of the students based life off of what they viewed on TV. For me that was very frustrating especially since I started attending the school during the wake of Hurricane Katrina. I was always taught to research and investigate information given to me. Figuring out and thinking about what a person or groups of people have to gain by giving you certain information and ultimately trying to alter your perception.

At OU I was strictly focused on graduating so I could find a job and make a little money. That's all I had in mind. I decided to get my Bachelor in Communication. The areas of communication I selected were Business Communication and Media Communication, which are two opposite ends of the spectrum. In my mind I was playing it safe as far as the major I was selecting. I totally suppressed my desire and need for the arts! I felt like it wasn't realistic anymore for me to pursue the arts. I had the mind frame of it will be a one in a million chance that I will be successful in the arts so why bother. I worked two jobs in the beginning of my college life but by the time I made it to Oakland University I only worked one job which, freed up a lot of time for me. I started to hangout more due to me being so close to graduating.

I was so thrilled when graduation finally arrived. All I could think about was the money that I was going to be making. The money I thought I was going to be making. What always makes me chuckle when I think back is my Father had me in a great financial position. I didn't have to pay any rent because he owned the home I was living in and paid my car note and insurance. I'm not sure why I was so pressed about money. After graduation I could not find a job! I graduated during the beginning of the recession in America. All of the major companies were laying people off, outsourcing work, moving their headquarters, or shutting down for good.

I was very frustrated about not being able to find a job. As I am sure you can imagine there were people with years of experience in Corporate America so naturally they were getting offers for jobs over new college graduates which I totally understand. After all I still had a job it just wasn't the job that I wanted. I didn't find a new job until September of 2008. I had previously taken multiple tests to get into the company and I passed every single test and still never got a call back. I went through some of my emails that I received from the company and found a number that I could call and actually talk to a live person. Before I called I said out loud yet quietly to the Universe "It would be great if I got a new job for my birthday." I called and was asked to proceed with the hiring process. I can't express to you how happy I was to move on to a new company and to gain true experience in the corporate world.

I was a workaholic! Not to mention I was pursuing my MBA. Now that I was working for a company full time I no longer really had time to do anything besides work, eat, and sleep. I made time to do my weekly 20 page papers of course. However, that isn't really living. I couldn't even take any vacation time until 6 months on the job. I worked a massive amount of over time, which I was not complaining about! I was doing what I wanted to do which, was to make more money. I was extremely comfortable with my work life. When I received my MBA I started to slowly look and apply for other positions within the company. I remember telling my boss at the time that I had just completed my Master's program and instead of her saying congratulations her reply was "Really? Bring it in!" I assume she didn't believe me.

How to Play the Game of Life

I started to really think about what I wanted to do with my life. I began to think about how I completely shut down all of my other interest that I felt weren't going to make me any money. I remember saying to myself in college that I never wanted to be stuck in a job that I did not like or couldn't see myself doing forever. I realized that I turned into the person that I didn't want to become. I felt stuck. Trapped!!! I still hadn't really figured out what it was I wanted to do with my life. I did realize that this was the first time in my life that I had never fostered any form of the arts! Can you imagine practicing some form of art your entire existence and then reach a certain point in your life and just never practice any art again? Even when I attended Oakland University I took theatre classes, published an article in the school newspaper, and took classes on voice recording and doing work within the radio station. I remember talking to my friend Bianca (Be Be) from high school and she was telling me how she was pursuing her acting career. I remember telling her how much I admired the fact that she was really chasing her dream! That is so commendable!

Knowing what you want is a gargantuan portion of life. I knew that I didn't want to attend Wayne State for college but I went anyway. I knew that my parents wouldn't be happy about me leaving Wayne

State to attend O.C.C. but I knew that was best for me at that time. I knew that I was suppressing my artistic side because I was afraid of failure. I was afraid of what people would think of me, how they would criticize my thoughts. In a world where social media allows people to say anything, getting feedback from other people can be terrifying. After a promotion to another department in my corporate work life I started to explore a little more on what I wanted to do artistically. I have always known that I had something to say and specific views and information on particular topics that were somewhat controversial. I would often express these views on my social media sites.

One day it hit me to start my own blog where I could verbally express myself in extensive detail. I contemplated on if I should create a website or not because I was afraid. I wasn't necessarily afraid of failing but more so of not being supported. I had to realize that even though I have a goal for my project I am pursuing writing to satisfy my soul. It's something that I wanted to achieve. I took my time researching other writers and asking my good friend Marcel Friday about purchasing a site and getting it set up. The more I inquired the more excited I became. Before I even purchased my site I had already written three blogs and had them proofread by my friend/editors Katrina and Ariel. I really wanted to be heard and for people to take what I was saying into consideration.

That was the birth of LetsTalkRaeStyle.com

I have also noticed in myself and in my circle of friends knowing what you want is also a huge part of dating (dating & relationships discussed in detail of Chapter 8) and friendships as well. Many women and men find themselves dating someone that isn't in the same league as them (GUILTY). I'm not saying don't give someone a chance just because he or she doesn't meet the requirements on your automatic checklist. I'm just advising you that four months in you know whether or not you two are on the same page. Women often settle or hit the snooze button on the alarm going off in their heads about the person or persons that they are dating. I personally am the Queen of dating. My good friend Lorri calls me a professional dater. It's kind of funny but then it's not. I have dated a lot just because I can truthfully. In a way dating different people helped me determine what I want and what I don't want. It's all about knowing yourself and what you can deal with; also, taking that time away from dating and analyzing the situations. Knowing yourself is so very important! There are so many lost souls walking around trying to look like everyone else. They are actually succeeding in looking like other people. Everyone seems to have the same hair, lipstick, style of dress, and fake personality. I'm not saying stand out I'm saying be who you are instead of being what's popular!

Most of my life I did what someone else wanted me to do. I went to a college that I didn't want to attend; I even majored in Business in Graduate school instead of getting a Master's in Psychology, which is what I really wanted. I sacrificed what I wanted to make other people happy or comfortable.

KNOW WHAT YOU WANT, GO AFTER WHAT YOU WANT, AND CONQUER WHAT YOU WANT!

Chapter 3

Depression

In the previous chapter I talked about being happy that I was graduating from Oakland University. Although I was happy about graduating I was sad at the same time. Three months before I walked across the stage my family and I lost the Matriarch of our family. My Granny. She had never been sick before and in December she began to have strokes and one day she just wasn't talking anymore. I still never considered that she would die. I had never even imagined life without her. I know that sounds strange but it really didn't cross my mind. She was my only living Grandparent. She was the only Grandparent I had ever known. I went to her house for every holiday. She's my Mother's mother, which is as close as you can get to your own Mother. My entire family was devastated. From that day on I knew that my family dynamics would never be the same.

I was under terrible emotional distress. To make matters worse I was already going through some emotional issues due to unnecessary stress. There were days that I would literally stay in the bed and cry. When I had to go to work I would put on sweat pants and a tee shirt with gym shoes. Anyone that knows me knows that I am super "girly." I love to dress up and I love makeup. I was totally out of character. Every time I would talk to my mother she would cry. I knew that it was hard for me but it was extremely difficult for my Mother. My Granny's oldest child. Leaving her as the Matriarch, a role that she wasn't ready for just yet. It's very difficult to be strong for one of the strongest people that you know. It all happened so soon. To this day I still don't know exactly what was the cause of death. What I do know is funerals and weddings bring out the worst in people. I know when my Grandfather died (Donald Goines) his Will was changed so that my Grand-mother's children wouldn't benefit from his books profits. The changes in the will are so blatant and obvious that it's almost unbelievable. It was changed so that my Grandfather's sisters and their children would reap all of the benefits financially and otherwise. What kind of people would cut out their own nieces and nephews to solely benefit themselves? To this day his children are still being cheated to what's rightfully theirs. When you lose a loved one people really show you who they are and what is really important to them. It was really important for her to see me graduate. I am her second oldest Grandchild out of about 35 Grandchildren. I still proceeded to graduate of course but I felt very empty.

I started to do some research on depression. There are technically two types of depression, which are Clinical Depression and Depression. Clinical Depression is a depression so severe as to be considered abnormal, either because of no obvious environmental causes, or because the reaction to unfortunate life circumstances is more intense or prolonged than would generally be expected (Dictionary.com)." Clinical depression has to be diagnosed by a professional. "Depression is defined as a condition of general emotional dejection and withdrawal; sadness greater and more prolonged than that warranted by an objective reason (Dictionary.com)." It's said that 17-20 million Americans suffer from depression and that suicide from depression is the second leading cause of death.

Only about 12% of African American women are noted as suffering from depression. That number is severely low because African American people con-

sider therapy to be weak or a means of saying someone is crazy when that is not the case. What happens
or at least what happened to me is that I became extremely moody. Some days I would wake up and just
cry. I didn't want to do anything. I would feel hopeless
or as if my life was so horrible. My depression was an
exaggeration of reality. Every situation seemed much
worse than it actually was. I did a lot of stress eating
and just eating because it was a form of comfort for
me. Eating made me more depressed because I already felt as if I had a weight issue. It's always surpris-
ing to me that I was totally conscious about over eating due to depression. I never sought therapy but I
wish I had because I could have come out of my depression much sooner.

My depression was off and on. I wasn't where
I thought I should be in life. I felt as if I worked hard
and my hard work wasn't paying off. I started to take
a turn for the worst by comparing my life with other
people's lives. Comparing your journey to someone
else's is not only ugly and a waste of time, but you
don't actually have a clue what the other person has
been through. You're on the outside looking into a
foggy window. My Father is the King of looking on the
brighter side. He started to tell me stories about his
life and the lives of people he knew and, how I should

be thanking my "lucky stars" (he always says that term) for the things that I do have.

Listening to the plight of the people you love will certainly help you bring your issues into perspective. I knew my Father was right but I had to believe that it totally applied to me and ultimately change the way I viewed my life. I had to decide that I could not let every event that happened in my life virtually destroy me or alter how I treat myself or other people. I wrote down everything in my life that I felt could be better and then I wrote down ways that I could make those things better in my life. I start thinking about how turmoil of some kind will always occur in life and, you just have to deal with those issues as they come along and focus on what I could control at that moment. I had to stop dwelling on the "Shoulda, coulda, woulda's." You can't change what has already happened; well at least you can't in this dimension or realm of the Universe. Try to move forward.

There is nothing wrong with seeking therapy. If you find yourself in a depressive state do what you must to ensure your mental health. Seeking professional help is not a sign of weakness, but recognizing that something is wrong is a sign of strength. Death may have initially started my depression but it was multiple factors that made depression linger on in my life. I have no real way of dealing with death. It's hard and we all have lost someone we love and that's going to continue to happen as long as we live. Maybe if we did receive professional help instead on internalizing everything therapy could help our healing process. We are only human and to survive the game of life we must find or try new ways to manage our pain.

Chapter 4

Motivation

Watching the interaction between parents and their children can be quite intriguing. When I talk to my friends that are Mothers/Fathers they speak with such determination and ambition. It seems as if people with children are always motivated. I think it's because Parents have little ones that totally depend on them for literally everything! The drive and determination seem to come from children. That in itself is motivating and often makes me feel like I should be able to do anything because all I have to be responsible for is myself.

It's said that most people are motivated by a desire to fulfill their needs. What if all your needs

have been met? What if you have a desire for something that you want and don't necessarily need? What
if you're just lacking motivation to perform your daily
tasks such as getting out of bed, going to work, or
working out? I am one of those people that constantly
motivate others. I don't care what situation the person that needs motivation is going through I can
make them feel better and empower them to make
changes for the better. When it comes to motivating
me, I often wonder where that good motivational
speech that I gave to someone else went?! It's like
looking in the mirror and seeing what I want right behind me, but my reflection shows me all the difficulties that I've experienced and the potential difficulties
to come. Seeing that reflection of myself makes me
not even want to try. It literally just makes me okay
with the way things are.

Whenever I lack motivation there are certain
people that almost always lift my spirits and make me
feel just a little bit better; my parents, sister and, my
aunt Timika. I can be extremely dramatic sometimes.
Okay I am dramatic but everyone is entitled to their
own feelings and emotions. Sometimes I have to motivate myself without them because no matter what
they say it's still all up to me. There are a couple of

things that I do to motivate myself. I look in the mirror and say positive things about myself, I give myself a pep talk, I watch TV, and listen to music.

It may sound vain, but saying nice statements to your self can be really helpful. People always say that I downplay myself, and my potential. Well I think the very same thing about other people. So let's just say that we as humans don't give ourselves our proper credit. This is not meant to be cocky or conceited. Tell yourself that you can do whatever your heart desires. Tell yourself that you are successful and that you are going to become more successful. While you're at it tell yourself that you are beautiful or handsome even if there are things that you would like to change about yourself. We all have flaws but we all must be appreciative for what we have and how we look. It really is important. Think about how many selfies you see a day on Instagram and Facebook. What do the captions say on those selfies? It's usually some cliché statement from a celebrity or TV personality like "She is Her," "You wish you could have me," etc. If you really read in between those lines it's usually a person trying to suppress their low self-esteem or just the insecurities they have.

How to Play the Game of Life

I'm not saying that those kinds of posts are bad. I'm just saying that a person with true confidence really doesn't have to say anything. Confidence will be oozing off of a person at the very sight of them.

THE PEP TALK

You have to be your own cheerleader! Encourage yourself! Pump yourself up! No one can make you do anything that you really don't want to do however, realizing that motivating oneself is a must. I don't want you to feel crazy so I suggest that you write down what you want to materialize in your life. Once you write them down you should write down ways that will help you achieve the needs or wants that you want to materialize. None of this is easy especially if you really do have obstacles holding you back. Financial freedom seems to be a booming topic. I hear people discussing how they want to buy homes and how they have student loans etc. I'm actually one of those people. I have student loans and let me tell you I have more student loans than I have degrees! However it was my choice to further my education. I have other binding financial responsibilities besides student loans and my monthly bills. There are two things that I try to keep in mind. The first thing is as long as you are alive you will always have some form of debt. The second thing is you can only conquer one thing at a time in its entirety. You can use those statements as motivation due to them both being very true. Tell yourself out loud what you want. If you want to become a healthier person tell yourself that you're going to be a healthier person. Talk yourself into getting what you want. It doesn't really matter how long it takes just as long as it's achieved.

THE IDIOT BOX (THE TV)

There is a love hate relationship with TV. It spews so much garbage on a regular basis that it can be confusing. Whenever watching TV try to keep an open mind. Watching certain shows make me laugh and forget about whatever problem I was going through. It really does take my mind off of some issues. Then there are shows that are positive and motivating. The ones that make you feel as if you can do anything. Those are really the shows you should watch if you're going to watch anything. I really like some of the worst shows that are shown on television. Shows that seem to be non-relatable to my life are the shows that I get the most enjoyment out of. If the show has lots of drama I seem to be all for it simply because it strays away from my own issues.

How to Play the Game of Life

MUSIC

Do you have songs from your childhood that makes you recall happy times and childhood memories? You know those old school songs that you hear and it turns you into a 7 year old all over again? Maybe the song makes you see yourself and what you were doing when you heard that song. I know I have a few songs that instantly bring on childhood memories. I learned at a young age that music can literally change how you're feeling. If a person is sad and then someone puts on Mary J. Blige's "My Life" album be prepared to comfort them and maybe even cry with them as well.

Whenever I'm in need for motivation I listen to songs that explain other people's problems. Now that may be strange but really it makes me think about how appreciative I should be for not having the particular problem that the artist is describing. The songs that make you realize that things could be worse. The music doesn't even have to be a specific genre. Tunes that are upbeat seem to be best when attempting to invoke motivation! You could call it feel good music! All musicians create some kind of feel good music. Music has the power to change a person's mood. Music is motivation!

Chapter 5

Changing Your Energy

Energy is INFINITE! It's all around you at all times. There are two definitions of energy that will be the focus of this chapter. The first definition of energy is the capacity of vigorous activity. The second definition is the ability to act, lead others, effect, etc., forcefully.

Your body is so important to any progress in your life. I always thought people were just trying to make me feel bad about my unhealthy eating choices. Well some people do just like to make others feel bad about their choices but others are just informing you for the greater good. I always feel tired. When I say I'm tired, people don't believe me because I have a desk job. However, my desk job is mentally draining.

How to Play the Game of Life

I previously worked in a call-center, which was extremely draining. Taking calls from different people and guessing what they want because many people can't accurately express themselves. No matter what field a person works in work can be draining. There was a point when I just wanted to eat and sleep. I didn't want to do anything extra.

There was also a period when I did want to become active but I was too exhausted to carry on with the plans. I started looking for ways to increase my energy. I probably just sound lazy but I had to make a decision and fast. In everyday life we all get tired but in order to remain active and participate in daily life you have to make some changes for yourself. I decided to decrease my gluttonous behavior, which was a difficult task because I love food, especially sugary snacks. Making an attempt to change my poor eating habits was a challenge. In fact it's still a challenge. I didn't get rid of anything major except for bread. I love bread. I love pasta! We know too much of anything can be a bad thing. The purpose of me eliminating bread was so I could eat foods that weren't as heavy. Eating foods that weren't extremely heavy made me feel better. I also started taking B12 vitamins. I started to hear lots of people talk about B12 shots. I'm not a fan of needles so that was never really an option for me.

Whenever looking for vitamins remember that liquid goes through your bloodstream faster. Consistency is everything when it comes to vitamins and other aspects of life and living. I incorporated more fruits and vegetables in my diet. When I say diet I don't mean restricting what I eat, I mean my regular food regiment. Fruits are very tricky for me because most fruits with skin make my throat, gums, and lips itch! Including apples, plums, cherries, and sometimes blueberries. I actually think it's the seeds in blueberries. What I like to do for breakfast or even a snack is create myself a smoothie using baby spinach leaves, strawberries, plain nonfat yogurt, blueberries or raspberries, with almond milk or orange juice. Blend those ingredients together and trust me it's very delicious but you're also getting vegetables and fruit directly in your body, right from your kitchen. Eating a salad everyday can increase your energy because of the amount of vegetables. Altering your eating can change your physical energy and help with mental clarity.

ENERGY TYPE NUMBER 2!

Have you ever felt like your energy was off with your friends and family? No one did anything to you personally, but the chemistry just didn't feel right within. Maybe you were battling emotions about a previous situation or relationship and you ended up displaying bad energy with people that didn't deserve the mistreatment. You have the ability to change and redirect your energy. Recognizing that your energy is off is all a part of truly knowing yourself (refer to chapter 7).

Have you ever walked into a room and immediately felt tension? Maybe you walked in and you couldn't describe the vibe that was currently in the room. My favorite scenario is when you enter an area and you feel that you were the topic of discussion before you walked into the room. Never let a situation alter your energy. Your energy has the capability to change everyone else's energy. You can change the aura! Walk into a room with positivity gleaming from your pores.

Do your best not to participate in energy draining conversations, like conversations that will question your motives and energy. It seems that whenever you are trying to keep your energy positive and at levels that are pleasing to you someone or something always tries to change your energy. You know the conversations that I'm talking about right? When one of your girlfriends dissecting someone else from head to toe or, when they start discussing a mutual friends flaws etc. and you're tempted to participate in the conversation and discuss what that person has done to you! It seems to be easy to get trapped into those conversations. I guarantee if you don't participate you won't be involved in any he said she said conversations either. No adult truly has time for that when dealing with real life! If it were a reality show then I can see that being an important factor.

Maintain your energy!

Chapter 6

Lost In Translation

Remember when all you had was a house phone and a pager? If someone called you at home and you weren't there they would page you. Maybe they had their own special code so you knew exactly who it was. 1-4-3 meant I love you and 3-0-4 was hoe, and 911 meant call me back now it's an emergency. I remember my sister and I had our own phone line and my Mother had her own. I used my Mom's most of the time because she really didn't talk on the phone. People usually just popped up at our house if they wanted to see or talk to her. I would be on the phone all night. I would watch TV while on the phone with my friend and they would be watching the same thing that I'm watching so we could discuss the show.

How to Play the Game of Life

How about when you and one of your friends got into an argument and you want to know what was said behind your back what would you do? Set up a three-way call of course so that you can press mute and see what she has to say about you. Do you remember your first three-way call? Everyone has tried to trip someone up at some point in time in their youth with a three way call. All of a sudden the phone game started to change because cell phones came along. Now the first cell phones were minute phones only! You only used the phone if it was a real emergency and had no other options. It was powered off at all times. I got my first cell phone for Christmas in the 8th grade. My family and I pulled names on Thanksgiving and my Uncle Michael pulled my name. I never thought in a million years he would get me a cell phone. His exact words were "I know you love to talk on the phone so I thought this was perfect for you!" I was soooo geeked! I can't even begin to explain how happy I was.

You have to understand a cell phone was not a common thing for a kid to have back then. Oh goodness did I say back then? I was the only one in my class with a cell phone! You couldn't tell me I wasn't the WOMAN. I would always make sure I had some minutes on it because there were no contracts! I'm excited just writing about the cell phone and that was 18 years ago! Of course cell phones started to become more common and then it was a cell phone epidemic! They were giving them away. Everyone had one and then here comes 2 way pagers. They were talking about 2 way pagers in all the rap songs. Displaying them all in videos because it was a way of messaging. I remember my Dad saying that my cell phone could do everything that 2 way pagers could do and he didn't understand why they were making such a big deal about them. Can you believe it? There was actually a time when your cell phone did not send text messages. You just made calls and left voicemails. Low and behold we are now in the era of text messaging, instant messaging, DMing, and inboxing all from our cell phones. We can communicate anyway we want to from our cell phones yet it seems that no one actually wants to talk on the phone anymore.

You can literally hold a text conversation with someone and decide to call them instead of continuing to text, then what do they do? Send you to voicemail and send you another message saying they can't talk right now. Yes they can! They just don't want to because everything has been made so, impersonal that we as humans have a difficult time with verbal communication. It's not that we don't know how to verbally communicate but we just don't feel like it or want to for some reason. I know when I'm at work and someone wants to call me instead of using instant messaging or emailing I immediately start thinking "What is it that they don't understand?" Why do I need to verbally deliver a message that I've already explained in writing? I get frustrated because I don't want to talk. When did this happen? I once loved to talk on the phone. Times have surely changed. It probably is best to verbally communicate at work because messages can easily be taken out of context especially when orders are being given.

I know the importance of verbally expressing my thoughts and feelings. How many times have you sent your home girl or boy a message and their response isn't applicable to what you originally sent? You're looking at the other person's message going "What?" What does that mean? I don't understand. Then you respond because there is no point in calling and now everything is all confused. All text messages are not created equally. So many of our messages get lost in translation because everyone's interpretations seem to be different. You have to know who you're texting. Some people are always multitasking so they half read your messages therefore their responses never make sense. Then you have the people that can't decipher between a serious message, a joking message, and a sarcastic message. They always respond defensively and you end up being confused yet again because you don't know what they are upset about. Have you ever sent someone a text message and they think you have an attitude because they have an attitude? That's always hilarious to me.

One thing I dislike about text messages is that they often are received out of the order in which they were sent. You'll be texting a thesis and you the recipient will be saying your messages are coming through out of sequence. Messages often get stuck while being sent. I had this one phone that sent all my messages out about 5 to 10 hours after I originally sent them. It was insane. Can you imagine getting a message that says "Let's do something tonight" at 2am? Totally sending out the wrong kind of message.

I miss the days where you would give out your number to someone you think is interesting or someone that you like and they would call you the next day. It was against the rules if they called you the same day they got your digits. You would be kind of excited. That's how you made it through the getting to know someone phase before you decided if you would let a guy take you out on a date. You know what people ask for now? Your phone number so they can text you and your Instagram name. They don't want to call you they want to text you. Then there are so many people that use this short hand texting or intentionally spell words incorrectly while texting for example NEWAY.

How to Play the Game of Life

Why in the hell can't you type out the word ANYWAY? If you're that lazy just maybe you should pick up the phone and call the person instead.

Instagram and Facebook are like super personal to people even though many people tell all of their business on those particular social media sites. A few of my friends make an effort not to follow anyone that they are dating on any social media sites and they don't allow the people they are dating to follow them either. In my mind it's because messages are mixed on social media and can translate to a reader as something totally different. I think a lot of that is because people have these facades on social media but when you're personally communicating with someone they are a different person altogether.

On Social media she's a model. Via text message she's asking you for a couple of dollars. You see how those things don't mix? What's real and what's fake? Some people try to act like they are just assholes on social media but in real life they really are assholes. Well at least they are being true to themselves unintentionally. If social media leaves you confused about who people really are and we're constantly texting people instead of talking to them even when we don't really know what they are trying to say it seems like verbal communication is somewhat dead or at least sick.

How are we going to be understood and understand others if we don't effectively communicate? Interpersonal communication seems to be a lost art. That's why so many people seem to be socially awkward in person. You always see people touching their phones and checking messages. I think restoring interpersonal communication is an essential part of life. You have to be able to communicate with people face to face. You have to be able to interview for a job in person. You have to be able to network in person. Most importantly you have to be able to verbally express your thoughts and feelings as well as understanding others. However, interpersonal communication works both ways. How uncomfortable is it trying to express your feelings to someone via messaging and they just never respond or when they do respond they don't address your statement or validate your feelings?

Important conversations shouldn't be texted. Pick up the phone and talk. Call someone over and talk in person. If you don't understand the message someone sent you pick up the phone and call them for clarity. If you don't want to end up being some weirdo that only exists online get out mix mingle and talk to people!

Chapter 7

Who's Around You?

I have been very fortunate to have the friends and associates that I have. I actually have lots of friends. I must say I have been in a situation where I have lost friends and each situation was quite disheartening. Sometimes we are blind to friendships and the motives of others. We all hope that our friends are happy for us, that they will support us when needed and just have good intentions. I'm guilty of letting some behaviors slide under my nose. In other words I consciously choose to ignore the behavior. At some point in the friendship I realized that this "Friend" would throw anyone under the bus to save their own behind. They didn't care what lies they made up as long as it helped them achieve whatever goal they were seeking at that moment which always happened to be a love interest.

I'm not sure what makes people continuously lie and then think that everyone should be fine with that behavior but I had to immediately and drastically cut the friendship off. Who needs or wants someone around them that truly has ill intentions? I hope no one. You want people around you that have the same intentions in the friendship as you.

I once had a friend that did absolutely nothing but borrow money from me and hang out with me. If I thought that I may not be able to loan her money she would say something like "You have it, or you can get it from your parents!" As if my parents just have money growing out of their ears! She was a longtime friend of mind. It was unfortunate that I didn't recognize her selfishness until it was too late. The fact of the matter is some people are just around when they are down and need assistance. When they are regaining stability they no longer need you. Better yet when they think they have found a meal ticket of some kind they find ways to exile you or accuse you of doing something that both of you know isn't true. You have to be very weary of people that think people owe them something.

Have you ever out-grown a friend? Perhaps, it was someone that you have been friends with since your childhood? People always ask why you don't talk to certain friends anymore and you may not have an actual explanation. Maybe you haven't taken the time to sit down and actually think about why you haven't talked to this friend. I try to hold on to friendships but sometimes you have to let people go! I outgrew one of my friends mentally in my freshmen year in high school. We weren't in any confrontation or anything we were just extremely mentally different. As we began to enter our late 20's we tried to see and talk to each other more because we were once very close friends. In fact we were Best friends. It became crystal clear why we were no longer so close.

It only takes a little while for people to show you who you they really are. I know that was very cliché but that is the truth. I'm not saying that all your friends have to think like you or be like you but to me if I can't hold a conversation with you without you getting upset because I don't agree with what you're saying it's really no point of conversing. That kind of behavior shows a lack of respect for others and their views. You simply can't grow with that mental state.

We choose our friends but we do not select our family. Some of us have back stabbing dirty family members. You know the ones that lie and start drama, exaggerate the truth all the time and that has to play the victim in every situation, often playing the devil's advocate. I'm sure you will always love your family but you don't have to have them around you. Some of us have family members that are attention whores. That's right I said it. The people that revert everything and every topic back to them. They are people just like everyone else. I always say to accept people for who they are but tolerate only what you can.

Surround yourself with people that have goals and initiatives. You want people around you that are interested in developing a circle or network of people to help reach goals. I'm always open to meeting new people. You never know what someone has to offer you as far as growth or business. I have always disliked the term "No new friends" which is a popular song but it's just a song and this book is about real life! In real life it's auspicious to engage with new people. I have noticed that many folks take whatever musical artist say to heart. I guarantee that they wouldn't have had much success if they completely isolated themselves from others. Connections are made by meeting friends or associates of your friends and, by going to different events and venues. I'm not suggesting that you immediately go out and make some random person your best friend, but what I am saying is staying in a bubble doesn't really perpetuate growth. Select the ones you want around you carefully especially if you do not possess a certain amount of acumen. My Mother has a great deal of acumen. When she first meets someone she can tell you if they are trust worthy. It's very similar to your parents being able to identify your fake friends before you can. My Mother can always tell you what the issues are or may be with a new person. Unfortunately, everyone does not have that insight upon meeting people.

Chapter 8

Heartbreak Hotel

Heartbreak is like a pain pulling at your heart that you can't quite describe to the doctor. It's astonishing that physical pain can be felt after an emotional break up.

SCENARIO 1

You're a 23 year old woman in what you call a loving relationship. You're supporting the dreams and aspirations of your man because that's what people do in relationships right? One day you wake up and you are all of a sudden in the rumor mill. You start getting messages about your man cheating on you. He's been caught red handed with a stripper and there are photos to prove it. You're crying your eyes out because you're in disbelief. Your mind is all over the place and the questions that you keep asking yourself are why? You keep asking what you did wrong. Why would the person you gave your heart to hurt you on purpose?

Most women mope around the house crying for days. Walking around like Wonder Woman without her cap feeling totally incomplete and damaged. They're crying because their heart has been broken and because deep down inside she's waiting for him to call and explain to her what happened. Even though you have evidence there is a small portion of you that wants him to text or call and say "It's not what it looks like." No matter what he says you won't feel better. After time passes on you realize that you can't be depressed forever so, you put on your best game face and tell your friends that you want to hang out tonight. Even though you aren't over your emotional distress you put on that dress that fits your body perfectly. All women have an outfit that makes them feel extra sexy. You and your girls head out. You all are posting pictures on Instagram just in case your ex is lurking through your page he'll see that you look good. Even though you had a good time with your friends you're still miserable.

The next day he texts you and asks what you're doing as if he didn't know you have been waiting on him to contact you. He admits his crime and asks if you all can be friends. A friend really just means he wants a revolving door into your life. The question now is do you let him? Hell no you don't! At least that's what your mind said but your heart agreed to the circumstances until.... Until you realized that his intentions were just to keep you around, while he continues to do whatever he wants, because, after all you're just friends. The decision has been made and you're done with him.

Now you're on a mission to move on and find someone new. You're going on dates and testing the waters. The minute that you come across a man that you think is willing to go along with your plan you're trying to force him in a relationship. Why: all because you don't want to be alone. You're busy thinking about all the women that your ex has been with and how easy it is for him to move on with someone new. Now you're heartbroken again because you've moved faster than this new guy wanted. Now you're trying to figure out why he lead you on when the truth is he didn't lead you on you lead yourself on.

SCENARIO 2

Maybe you're the woman that has decided to give a chance to a certain type of man that you normally wouldn't date. You know, you're the one that has a list of characteristics or at the very least standards, but none of the men that met the requirements have been "the one." You come across a man that looks decent, has a good job, and he speaks your language about family and love. He doesn't meet all of your standards but you're giving it a try anyway. You decided to overlook the things that you can't change, like the fact that he has 5 kids with 4 different women. It's been 8 months since you all started dating. He treats you well and he takes care of all of his kids. That seems to work out well until he proposes to you, which is exactly what you wanted. You want the happily ever after. He loves you and this is the first proposal you ever received. Dating outside of your normal type guys was a great idea.

You immediately announce to the world i.e. Facebook that you're getting married. You even posted a picture of your ring. You call all of your friends to let them know the first meeting to plan the wedding is next week. Everything is perfect until..... The bad behavior begins. All of a sudden he doesn't answer his phone like he normally would. He's never at home and when you come by on your lunch break he isn't there either. The mind then starts going crazy. All kinds of scenarios start playing in your head. When you do speak with him you ask him what's been going on. He gives you the excuse of "I just been tired from working overtime," which is understandable. One night you decide you're going to stay a few nights. His phone keeps ringing in the middle of the night he looks at it and ignores the calls. He says that it's his youngest child's mother and that she doesn't want anything.

He doesn't know that you're inspector gadget and that you'll find out everything you need to know. Since he doesn't have a lock on his phone you're going to wait until he's well passed the r.e.m. stage of sleep and take a look for yourself. As the old saying goes "What you seek you shall find." Once that phone is opened and the truth is revealed that he is obviously still emotionally and sexually involved with the Mother of his child the feeling of brokenness and re-gret start to rush over your mind and body. How dare he do something like this to you when you gave him a chance? He should have been appreciative to have a woman like you!

SCENARIO 3

You've been dating this guy for a few months and you know he's the one. You two have done every-thing already and you get a long wonderfully. He has some education under his belt, he's well known, and you really like him. You even cater to him in multiple ways because you make more money than he does. Even though he didn't get you anything for Valentine's Day it's not a big deal. He's basically your man without the title. He always apologizes when he does something you don't like and you love that about him so there are never any arguments between the two of you. One day he tells you that he's going to be out of town for the weekend so he won't be able to see you. No big deal.

You decide to get on Instagram and you just happen to get on "your man's" Instagram page and you see pictures of him in very familiar locations. Maybe these are old pictures that he's reposted because he's out of town. You decide to call him and of course he sends you straight to voicemail. Are those old pictures? Is he out of town? Why isn't he answering the phone? What is he doing? You continue to watch for posts from him because he can't help but show all that he's doing. As the pictures keep coming it becomes apparent that he is not out of town. He's in the same state that you're in and he seems to be celebrating with a girl and another couple. This is when you turn stalkerish and the text messages begin. You start sending a thesis via text about how you know he's not out of town and how he needs to explain himself because you want to know whom he's with. You're furious.

He waits a while to contact you back to let you know that he is technically out of town. He's still in the same state as you but in a different city. He claims that he is celebrating his "friends" promotion at her new job. The friend is the unidentified woman that you saw in the picture. He tells you he'll talk to you later and doesn't text or call you for the rest of the weekend. Now you're blowing up his phone to no avail. He's not answering or responding to the 10,000 text messages you've sent him. When he finally does contact you his demeanor is nonchalant. He's acting as if he doesn't really want to be bothered with you, so you change your tune to accommodate him. You don't want him to act as if he doesn't care. You just want to know what's going on with him.

Only when he decides he is ready to tell you everything is when he talks. After he tells you the truth about this girl being his actual girlfriend and he's been seeing you both instead of you dropping him you turn the situation into a competition. You want to compete for a man's heart even though he just told you that he had a woman. You want to prove that you really are right for him and that he can be himself when he's with you. You continue to cook for him, provide whatever he needs financially; you give your body and soul to him as if nothing has changed. However, it eats you up knowing that he's with his girlfriend when he's not with you. The situation has gone too far and now both women know about one another. His girlfriend decides that she will not stand for his nonsense and dumps him. Congratulations you're the only one left. You won! However, is a win by default a real win?

THE ASSESSMENT

In scenario one attempting to be friends with someone that you are still very much so emotionally attached to is a bad idea. It's not only bad but it's selfish on behalf of the person that suggested the immediate friendship. It's not being fair or considerate of the emotional state that the woman is experiencing. It's always a good idea to try and get out the house after days, weeks, and sometimes months of hibernating after a breakup. Yet, you can't be on a mission to find a new man. I have heard women say "the best way to get over a man is to get under a new one." Now I'm not judging anyone that practices that model but I don't understand the notion. How could you possibly find a new man when you're not even over the most recent one? I can understand dating or just getting to know people. However, consider the fact that you may be setting yourself up for failure. All heartbreak deserves and desires healing but it seems we don't want to deal with our raw emotions.

What bothers me is that we as women constantly want to place blame on ourselves for the actions of others. "What did I do wrong?" Wasn't I enough?" "How did I make him unhappy with me?" "I drove him away." Just maybe you didn't do anything wrong. If you can't make a person be faithful you can't make them cheat either. There is no sense in blaming yourself: It'll only make you feel worse about the situation and ultimately lowering your self-esteem. You'll start to name all these ridiculous details about yourself that you don't like and you'll go downhill from that moment.

In scenario two lowering your standards, expectations, or criteria does not mean that you're going to strike gold in the relationship department. Wait! Why would you want to date a man that has 5 children with a bunch of different women? Doesn't that tell you a small portion about him and his behavior when it comes to women and relationships? I have a small news flash for you. Just because you think you're more accomplished than the person that you're dating doesn't mean he or she will treat you that way. YOU ARE NOT SPECIAL! I mean that in the most positive way ever. I mean you aren't more special than the four women that he has children with. I'm sure they wanted to be with him and one or more of them probably still want a relationship with him. You can't expect to be treated differently than the rest.

There are just so many possible issues with this situation. I don't even think an average working person can financially support 5 children. Without even looking at the financial aspect the relationship would be a challenge just on dealing with the Mothers of his children and coordinating time, budgets, holiday's, etc. Is 8 months enough time to determine you want to spend the rest of your life with someone? I'm a person that doesn't necessarily believe you can put a time frame on love. When you feel that the person is right for you go with the flow if the feelings are mutual: However, when the person starts displaying unusual behavior patterns, that's a red flag.

Scenario three is a case of being misled. It happens to the best of us but how the situation plays out just depends on what you allow or are willing to accept. Giving all of yourself away in the very beginning is a mistake. I don't mean sexually. I mean emotionally, spiritually, etc. Leave some mystery it's needed. No one needs to know your every move, not even the person you're seeing. Many relationships fail due to financial issues. Just because you make more money than your "man" doesn't mean you have to foot the bill all the time or not expect a gift on Valentine's Day. Recognize when you're being used.

Referring to someone as "your man" can be awkward. It's only awkward because there are so many people claiming men but those same men aren't claiming those women. Before you go putting a title on a relationship maybe you should actually have a conversation to determine if you're really in a relationship. Once it's determined that you aren't the only woman, and that's what you were led to believe, then you have been deceived, period! When you make the conscious decision to still date that person and continue on as if nothing happened then you deserve whatever he throws your way. I say that because you should not be willing to share someone just to save face. You shouldn't have to share simply because you don't want to.

Hanging on until the other woman decides she's done is not winning! That is a win by default. The other woman knew that she deserved more. She deserved better and the question is why didn't you think more of yourself? Now it's just you and him, but you don't trust him so you need to know his every move at all times. You don't want him to hang out with his friends or go anywhere that you aren't attending. Whenever he goes somewhere without you you're blowing up his phone. This is what you wanted because this comes along with being with him. Never allow yourself to be so consumed with another person that you lose sight of who you are and what you deserve. Don't expect a person to change when they have already shown you who they are and you accepted them.

Not knowing what love is was displayed in all three scenarios. Love yourself. Be the best person that you can be when you're single and in a relationship. Do your part as far as growing and being committed within a relationship but it's important to recognize when those same attributes aren't being given to you. Understand that it's okay to be alone. I think there are lots of women and men that have missed the person that they are supposed to be with because they are wasting their time in treacherous relationships.

I have sought out my older female friends for advice about men and relationships and I've heard so many times that I'll have to deal with cheating. I was told that I'll just have to ignore it because basically no man is perfect. No woman is perfect either yet monogamy shouldn't be up for question or bargaining. I have come to the realization that the women and men that just accept infidelity don't think they can find someone that wants just them.

Some people are in relationships because they need a place to stay. Others are in relationships because it's beneficial and or convenient. Be patient enough to wait for the real McCoy of love. It'll be worth the wait.

Chapter 9

Power

I want you to know that you have POWER! You were born with power! Sometimes other people can see the power within someone else and try to stomp all over it because they know the other person doesn't recognize the power within them. I have witnessed women and men within relationships allow their significant other to take their power. I don't mean power as in dominating the relationship I mean power as in self-worth and not allowing others to demean them especially in front of others. I have witnessed a woman in a relationship totally degrade her spouse verbally as if he wasn't a man or a human. I'm sure she knew subconsciously that what she was doing was wrong but since he allowed it she continued on with the behavior. That's an example of letting someone stomp all over your power because you don't recognize the power that you have within yourself. If he recognized his power that kind of behavior wouldn't stand because his spouse would already know that her actions were unacceptable.

Recognizing the power that you possess can possibly change your life. Have you ever wondered how you and someone else can have the same exact problem or issue and you're stressing about it and they are continuing on with life as if nothing ever happened? Maybe you are seeing them overcoming their issues step by step. You start to wonder how is it that they are progressing and you aren't. The reason is kind of simple but it's difficult to attain all at the same time. Your power goes along with battling a negative mind-set verses a positive mind-set. Use the power of your mind to create solutions in overcoming your obstacles.

For example there are so many well educated people in the world that are not generating enough income to maintain their daily lives and also to do extra activities such as vacation, shop, etc. Well educated doesn't mean that you went to college it means that you have knowledge of many things and you know how to coexist in a world that isn't always fair. That's my definition of educated. However, if you did attend college you may have student loans. Student loans are something that plague many college student and graduates. Not to mention some people have student loans and children/families. It seems like whatever money you make is never enough when it comes to paying bills and taking care of your other responsibilities. Let's say for example Jessica and Crystal both live on their own, they both make 40k a year, and they both have debts to pay off that seem impossible to do especially since they have rent/mortgages, car notes, insurance, water bills, electricity, and whatever other necessities they have. Crystal gets extremely upset about life and how she wishes she never went to college. Crystal knows that she deserves a higher paying job and just wishes she had a better life altogether. Jessica on the other hand is attempting to find new ways to generate more income so that she can do things that she wants to do and still be able to pay her bills.

Jessica is using her power of being and desire to overcome what many people suffer from which is debt. Jessica understands that she has the ability to change how the situation affects her by using her mental power to keep moving forward. We are faced with so much imagery of bull shit on a daily basis as far as what successful people look like. We often compare ourselves with those images of people. That's giving the media power to determine your success!

How to Play the Game of Life

Everyone knows someone like Crystal. It's not that Crystal wants to be this way but she hasn't discovered how to use her mental power. Crystal is one of those people that compares her life to the life of a reality star. Crystal doesn't understand that there's a reason why certain images are glorified on television. The reason is to make you subconsciously feel a certain way about yourself that isn't necessarily good.

What Crystal doesn't realize is that she has the power to change her circumstances. Sometimes we are just overwhelmed with emotions of anger and stress that we can't think clearly. We get so wrapped up mentally that we end up suppressing our power. We often start to create problems in our mind that don't even exist. That's called over thinking which is a sure way to lose your own power that is stored in the same area where your over thinking begins. Let your power take over and lead in a way that will help you in life not hinder you.

Use your power to guide you.

Chapter 10

Beware of your actions. (Learned Behavior)

I once knew a lady named Sherry. Sherry had a husband named Alex and two children, two daughters to be exact, Tiffany and Tammy. They had been together since I was a child. In fact my Mother was even in their wedding. I knew them before they even had children together. They were family friends. Sherry always complained about her husband to her friends. She talked about him not having money and even discussed his hygiene challenges. She's one of those people that apparently talked too much.

Sherry and her husband seemed like a decent stable couple looking in from the outside. They were the couple that always had card parties inviting friends over for a good time. It was becoming painfully obvious that Sherry was very tired of her situation with her husband. One day Sherry decided to kick her husband out just out of the blue and began dating her husband's best-friend. Is it me or does this sound like a great blues song in the making? Not only did she date her husband's best-friend but a year later they got married. Sherry's children are now calling this man Dad whom they used to call uncle.

Tiffany is now an adult and trying to find her way through life and most importantly to love. Tiffany is one of those young girls that constantly post pictures of food she's cooked explaining how she's going to be a great wife to someone one day. She adores the attention that she receives from people when she talks about being lonely and not having a man. When she does have a man or likes someone she's quick to check her friends about talking to him or being cordial. One day Tiffany caught the eye of a man that should have been forbidden fruit on the grounds of common sense not to mention girl code. Tiffany decides to sleep with her cousin's boyfriend. Of course she didn't really think anyone would find out. At least they wouldn't find out until they were in a relationship together. Once she realized that she was being shunned from the family for her actions she decided it would be best to let go.

It's evident that Tiffany didn't think anything was wrong with her rambunctious behavior. I mean her mother did something very similar so I'm sure she was hoping things would work out in her favor as well. When your Uncle becomes your Dad I expect there to be some misconceptions about relationships in a person's mind. Be careful what behavior you display in front of your children. Most parents don't want their children following in their footsteps. They want their children to make better choices. In this particular case she should have lead by example.

My parents are total opposites. My Mother is fiery and flirty. My Daddy is level headed and logical. I'm still unsure of how they actually got together. They had very different tactics when it came to disciplining my sister and I. My mother would overreact. She yelled, cursed, and even whooped us sometimes. In my case yelling was enough to burst out into tears (sensitive child). My Daddy on the other hand would make us verbally describe why we made a bad decision, which was so aggravating. He also did something called drills. Drills were completely embarrassing. He would give you commands and you would have to follow them until he got tired of telling you what to do. For example "Stand up, sit down, stand up, sit down." I almost forgot about those book reports and punishments from dear old Dad. My mother almost never stuck to her punishment rules.

Have you ever thought about how you come to the decisions of which you have made? How you react to certain situations? I know I can be cool as a cucumber at times and then other times I'm a firecracker that doesn't need to be lit. I can be filled with melancholy or my feelings can be nonexistent. Sometimes I want to talk about the issue that may be occurring for a couple of reasons; one is because I want to be heard and I want the other party to communicate with me, and the other reason is because I may want to make someone feel bad. Well not exactly feel bad but when you hear someone else describe your actions sometimes it helps the other person see how right or wrong they had been.

My mother can be extremely mean and evil, and my Daddy can be a sarcastic, belittling, something or another. Those are the traits that I dislike about my parents the most. My sister Amber and I always talk about that and laugh. Something that my Daddy always told us "Be careful about what you say you don't like because you'll find yourself behaving the same way." I find myself getting upset about simple things or becoming annoyed easily. I often find myself explaining things to adults as if they are children. Those are things that I didn't like that my parents did. I literally have to check myself about my behavior because I don't want to display the actions of my parents that I do not like. It seems to be pretty easy to adopt the behavior of your parents or who ever raised you.

Sometimes behavior can have the total opposite effect. For as long as I can remember as a child my mother would come in my room and give me hugs and kisses in my sleep. She would literally say "Ashley I love you" over and over again and I would always wake up because her loving raspy voice would seep through to my dreams. She was always very affectionate. I remember asking her why she always does that and she explained to me that her mother wasn't affectionate. She didn't give out hugs and kisses often and didn't say I love you that much. When my Mom had kids she made a decision that she wanted to show and express her love often. My mother made a decision to do the complete opposite of what her Mother displayed to her. She made an effort to do things differently. That has always been intriguing to me.

How to Play the Game of Life

WHEN TRAGEDY STRIKES

Do you remember the first tragedy that occurred within your family that you were old enough to comprehend? I remember mine. It was when my baby cousin who we lovingly called "The Dude (Donald Goines III)" died. I was six years old. I recall being awakened from a deep sleep by my Mother telling me to get up and that we were going to my Granny's. On the way to Granny's house my Mother explained to me that the Dude had died. From what I can recall my Mother was freaking out. Rightfully so, he was only three years old. It was devastating. I wasn't allowed to attend the funeral because my Mother felt I was too young.

After that my entire family started playing the blame game. I'm still not sure if that's something that all families do but we sure did. People stopped talking to each other for a while. Family functions weren't the same. However, that didn't last very long. The point was it happened. We actually had a feud with another family because of this. I'm talking about a real life Montagues and Capulets family quarrel.

This is a small example of how bad it got. It was so bad that a teenager from my family got into a physical altercation with a teenager from the other family just for walking down the street. I mean that, literally walking down the street. After the fight was over the teenager from my family said "That's okay because I'll be back with my Mother and my Auntie and we're going to have a party!" When she returned with her Mother and Aunt her Mother took a lock and launched it through the front picture window as a message. It's kind of weird reflecting on these events because things could have gotten progressively worse. Thank goodness it didn't.

All of those events should have been handled differently. Instead of blaming one another we should have been supporting one another especially to the parents of the Dude. They needed the most support and understanding. We seem to let our minds play tricks on us when we are at extreme lows in life. We make our loved ones our enemies when they are actually on our side.

The teenagers fighting are a perfect example of keeping children in their place. The initiator of the fight could have prevented everything that happened if she just kept her mouth closed. She knew our families were at war and she wanted to poor gasoline on the fire. She was the cause of her window being broken. However, it should have never come to that point because the parents should have been able to have a conversation regarding what took place. The conversation shouldn't have escalated the situation.

Chapter 11

The Pressure

Everywhere I turn there is some sort of advertisement telling me what I need to do or have. According to society I should be driving a Subaru, married, have 2.5 children, manageable student loans, do yoga, cook on a regular basis, have already experimented with my dreams, and wakeup in the morning with fresh makeup on. Not to mention if I'm not married I'm supposed to be desperate to get married and also there is something wrong with me either physically or emotionally because I'm not married. Can you all give a gal a break?

How to Play the Game of Life

FRIENDS

In my late 20's I decided to make-up for all the partying that I had missed due to trying to focus in school and when I was trying to be a "good girlfriend." I'm at the age in life where my friendship dynamics have started to shift. I'm going to say from ages 27 to 30 I went absolutely good time crazy. I think that was the most fun. If it wasn't a trip, road trip, full vacation, or a regular weekend outing going on, it was a serious problem for me. Having good times with friends and/or family was an absolute necessity. When you get tired of hanging out you'll have something to reminisce about. Although my hanging out days are not completely over they have slowed down drastically. I'm very particular about what venues and events I wish to attend. I'm concerned about the cost because I could be saving the money that I'm spending on going out. Which one of my friends am I bringing with me? All friends are not equal in the matter of going out because there are always one or two that can't control themselves especially when alcohol is involved. It's just a lot of things to consider when hanging out now.

More of my friends are settling down in relationships. Some are moving in with their mates, some getting married, and others are having children. Life as we knew it has been changing and evolving. Let me tell you it is a beautiful thing to watch your friend marry the love of her life. Some of my friends are excelling in their careers, and as people. With all these wonderful things going on there are always going to be those people that constantly try to make you feel as if your life is missing something because you may not be advancing in the same area in which they are advancing. You know that friend that wants you to be pregnant with them? They ask you because they may be on child number two or three "When are you going to have a baby?" It's not just your friends it's your family too. "When are you going to have a baby?" Not "do you want kids? Not "Do you want to get married?" They don't even ask you in what order or if you want either one. They just think that by a certain age women are supposed to have children. It usually takes place in the 20's age bracket. I always thought that women fought to do more than get married and have children. Not that there is anything wrong with being married or having children. I think they are both amazing. However are those the only great accomplishments for women in the eyes of most? Have you not achieved anything in life as a woman if you aren't married or have children?

Do people actually think about the words they say or how they could be making someone else feel?

How to Play the Game of Life

Let me give you an example of how these interactions sound. Be sure to read this out loud

> **Megan**: "Hey Lisa how are you?"
>
> **Lisa**: "I'm great! I just started a new clothing line and got a promotion at my job. I'm also trying to put together a networking group."
>
> **Megan**: "That's good how old are you now?"
>
> **Lisa**: "I'm 29."
>
> **Megan**: "Wow, when are you going to have some kids? It's going to be too late in a minute."

Do you understand how that sounds to Lisa? Megan just pissed all over Lisa's accomplishments by basically telling her that she hasn't actually done a thing because she still doesn't have children. Somehow in Megan's mind everything that Lisa said equated to nothing. I wonder if it ever crossed Megan's mind that Lisa may not be able to have children. The same thing goes for women in business. How dare you ask a Mother and wife if she wants something more than being a stay at home Mom? As if that isn't a difficult job. My question is why are we so quick to push people in the boxes that we think they should be in? Why don't we allow people to follow their own paths?

Lisa probably went home feeling like she's failing in life. Some women have a plan for how they want that sector of their lives to play out. Some women want to be married at least two years before they have children so that they can enjoy being husband and wife before they bring another person in the relationship. Some women don't want to have children at all. Some women are just free spirits and feel as if it's meant for them to reproduce then it will happen. No need to plan such an event unless that's what you want.

THE FAMILY

I love getting together with my family on holidays! I'm always excited to see who's going to come, what's on the holiday menu and just catch up with every-one. We all have lives and responsibilities, so getting together is a break from the regular routine. Then we do what all families do which is swap stories about work, the people we work with, and of course tell jokes about how we really wanted to handle different situations. What do you do when your family starts to ask the questions of when are you getting married or when are you going to have a baby? Just tell them to support you on your current endeavors and if and when you decide to have children or get married they will be the first to know. Unfortunately, I have to answer these questions often and I'm not even sure why. It's not like lots of people in my family are married anyway. Remember to stay out of the ovaries of others.

I hope this chapter helped you realize that you don't have to feel pressured by people that think they know what you want or think they know what your life is missing. It doesn't matter who they are. If you're a stay at home Mom and you love what you're doing then by all means continue to raise your child or children and, remember that your job is being responsible for the development of human beings! That is extraordinary. If you're in the corporate world and you're striving to continue to climb that ladder remember to carry a flat pair of shoes when your feet start to hurt. If you're an entrepreneur trying to become the next big thing, try to find ways to fund yourself so all the money you make truly is your money. To college students everywhere you can create your own lifestyle and remember that a degree just adds to your accomplishments it doesn't guaranty you anything.

Chapter 12

Karma

I have been hearing about Karma long before I actually knew what karma meant. Even though the word karma comes from Hinduism or Buddhism many people are believers in karma. Some people say, "What goes around comes around." "You reap what you sow." People also talk about getting back what you put into the Universe. All of the terms have the same message. I am a believer of karma to a certain extent. For example if you've stolen from someone you may or may not have known, I would expect that the Universe would bring some of that energy back around to you. I mean that would be reaping what you sow.

How to Play the Game of Life

It seems that karma doesn't always come back around in the way in which the action was distributed. I watched someone's successful professional career diminish in a matter of three months or so. It wasn't that they weren't great in their profession. I truly believe it was their karma for being evil, deceitful, and disrespectful to someone that didn't deserve that treatment. That's the form that karma took that you wouldn't necessarily expect to occur, do to the mistreatment of a person, well at least I wouldn't. I would think that someone they loved and cared about would just mistreat them in return but, since karma is more like an energy than something tangible I suppose you just don't know in what form it will evolve.

Do you know someone that you consider to be a bad person? Maybe they aren't a bad person, suppose they just have lots of scumbag actions. You always wonder about their karma. When are they going to get their payback? You get your karma back immediately (so you think). It seems that we are always looking for others to get what we think they deserve yet we're oblivious to why certain incidents are happening to us. It seems that when it comes to internal searching many of us fall short. We don't think whatever we have done was bad enough to get whatever karma we're currently experiencing. We often have a much different picture painted of ourselves than what the actual picture displays.

I once read that it's not up to humans to decide what we think our karma should be or anyone else's because we don't know what has been worked out in the Universe or in a past life that is beyond this realm or dimension of the Universe. The reading provided an example of a child dying. It discussed how we automatically think about how children are innocent and don't deserve to be harmed. It went on to say that it's not our job or place to even make that assumption. It hinted around the parents or one of the parents may have worked something out in a past life and the child 's death was the payment of karma. That is where I kind of draw the line in my belief of karma. It definitely made me think. I've actually heard my mother say something very similar. "Children pay for the sins of their parents." Daughters pay for the sins of their Fathers." Those are actual sayings from my Mother. I remember there was a tragic death of a young woman and I said that's so horrible she didn't deserve that. My Mother said: "You don't know what her parents may have done to someone." My Mother virtually described the same thing as the book but she used different terminology. I personally think that terrible things often happen to people just because;

everything isn't always good in life. Good doesn't even exist without bad. They coexist together.

If your karma is based upon your current actions and your parents past and current actions do you really know what to expect from karma? The good and bad karma both affect how you navigate and succeed in life. Our actions determine a portion of our destiny or fate. If you went to work and were treated poorly by your boss on a regular basis and then turned around and treated your team poorly you're just feeding bad forms of karma that will eventually come back to you. If you reacted to your team with kindness because that's how you desire to be treated then some form of kindness will return back to you. You and your reactions are the only things that you can control. I think if you consider all the good that you desire to come into your life and produce that same goodness in the Universe then it will be returned.

Think before you react. Reflect on ones self before you decide what you don't deserve. Be the goodwill that you desire.

Chapter 13

Spirituality and Peace

Spirituality can be such a touchy subject that it's sometimes uncomfortable for me to talk about. However, I find that it's extremely important and goes along perfectly with the previous chapters of this book. Although I have been to a few different churches I have never needed an ecclesiastic to inform me of what I felt around me, in heart, or what was right or wrong. My Mother has always been very vocal about spirits that she had come in contact with over the years and mostly in her childhood so, I always knew that spirits exist and are all around us. In fact I think I was about 6 years old when I told my Grandmother that I was playing with my younger cousin that had passed away. Growing up with family members that come from a variety of Religious backgrounds from Catholics to Agnostics and, from Atheist to Seventh day Adventist; I was always given the information I asked for on different Religious belief systems. I appreciate that so much because there are so many people that are told that they shouldn't ask questions because that's questioning God. In all actuality it's just questions that you want to know simply because your brain formed them. To be perfectly honest I think people give the response of "You don't question God" because they don't know the answer and or someone told them that when they asked a question.

Here is what it all boils down to for me. I do not believe in structuralized Religion but I do believe in God or Gods for that matter. I'm not writing this to attempt to change the minds of anyone. I'm just giving my perspective and my beliefs. Most Religions are based off one another or tell very similar stories and yet people of different Religious backgrounds think that others are wrong or even evil for not believing in the same religious sector that they believe in. I will never understand that. I also don't think that people can have true peace if they carry on those types of attitudes. I'm here to tell you that no matter what your belief is you are not wrong for that belief! How could you be? It's your belief and your Faith! I consider myself to be somewhat a spiritualist if I must put it in a category. I prefer not to categorize or label myself any further than the world has already done for me. I believe that God is everything around you and most present in forms that can't be seen.

The reality is this no matter if you're a Catholic, Baptist, Muslim, or Hebrew when you pray for something and your prayer is answered it's because your conscious and subconscious are working together. They are connecting to the Universe and energy that is all around us daily. You are connecting your highest self to God. Your belief and mental acceptance work together to form what your heart truly desires. An answered prayer is the realization of what your heart desires. It doesn't matter what your religion is, what creed you are, or what ethnicity you represent. Your prayers can be answered.

Moving along to peace within spirituality. Everyone seems to be so busy nowadays. I totally understand why many of us work for corporations that demand most of your time. Some people work multiple jobs and manage to do volunteer work as well. When your alarm starts screaming at you to get out of bed and start your day remember to take a moment for your self before you get out of the bed. Just lay there for a moment to fully awaken and to think about how you would like this new day to flow. You can take the time to pray or meditate or whatever it is that you want to do.

Just be sure to give yourself some time first thing before you start your day of doing things for others because that's pretty much what you do at work. Even if you work for yourself you're providing some sort of service to someone else. Doing so can bring on an overall calming and peace like aura for you and can last the rest of the day. Forget about who upset you yesterday or last night. Don't hold on to things of that nature. That's something that I have worked on and that I'm still working on. I often get upset when people don't follow through with tasks or obligations that they originally agreed upon. That's really just how some people are. Some are repeat offenders some aren't. Sometimes I just feel like that's how people are period!

If I or anyone else spent time on finding ways to retaliate against a person or persons, what exactly would that change? They still disappointed me, so that doesn't change and they probably don't even think what they did was a big deal. It's no way that I can have any peace if I continuously allow let downs or expectations of others to shake me up. We are all works in progress. We should all try not to do things to people that we don't want done to us or to our children or loved ones. I always try to keep that in mind with my day-to-day interactions with people. To achieve true peace you have to accept the unchangeable. Let go of what you can't control. Most importantly be able to sleep at night with the decisions you have made for yourself.

Chapter 14

An Open Mind

Have you ever been standing in line at the market and overheard a conversation about Caitlyn or Laverne (Transgender women)? Well I have. I really hate to eavesdrop but if I can hear I'm going to listen. I have heard the most obscene comments especially about Caitlyn that I have ever heard in my life. Please know that I understand it's a delicate situation and all of society may not be ready for it, but it happened. To be honest you don't have to like it or agree with the topic. However, you should always be respectful to others no matter who they are. You never know who is around you and whom you may be offending. I always try to think about how others must feel especially in situations I don't necessarily understand. I mean we can barely get people to recognize African

How to Play the Game of Life

Americans as Human Beings so I know we have an extremely long road ahead.

Some people often use the excuse of "I wasn't raised that way," in an attempt to be bigots. Just because you were taught certain things as a child, doesn't mean that what you were taught was right or the truth. Parents do the best they can, based on how they were taught. Many people were taught about Santa Claus, The Tooth Fairy, and the Easter Bunny. However, none of those stories are true. They are just a way to open the minds of children to imagination. Also to get parents to buy toys, candy, baskets, and give money for their children losing a tooth! You could take that as your parents raised you to lie to your kids. That may be a little extreme but I'm just giving you a different way that those stories can be perceived.

With so many differences between people, it is imperative to remain somewhat open minded. Being open minded doesn't mean that you have to accept things that you don't agree with, but attempt to see the situation from another's point of view. A massive part of being open-minded is not to jump to conclusions and make irrational assumptions. Many of us often live in a bubble or have limited contact with others that can't necessarily relate to our experiences.

When we do come across individuals that eat differently than we do or have different morals than we have, we pass judgment quickly. It's probably not intentional I think it's the way some of us are programmed. You could be missing out on a new friend, knowledge, and new experiences by remaining close-minded. I think the most valuable portion of being open-minded is knowledge. You have to be able to see things through a different perspective. Views, opinions, and even facts change (depending upon new discoveries and information). Seeing different perspectives can add value to your life.

A key element to being open-minded is to be open with ones self. Being open with your self is to be appreciative for waking up to a new day. Instead of being upset that you have to work think of it as another opportunity to feed yourself and your family. That's a perspective I believe we all can live with. A new day is truly an opportunity. Trying new adventures is another way to become open-minded. You could try new foods, travel to new places, new events, and new activities. People are quick to say what they don't like yet they have never even tried it to make an accurate decision. There was a time when everyone hated sushi! Now everyone loves some type of sushi because they were daring enough to give it a try.

How to Play the Game of Life

Embracing the unknown doesn't have to be drastic. You could start off slow by doing something simple like taking a different route to the gym. Maybe someone has been hinting around about going on a date together. Instead of pretending you didn't comprehend the innuendo take the initiative and set an actual date. Start saying yes to things you usually would decline. The next time you say no to something think about what triggered you to say no. It could be fear or the lack of wanting to step out of your comfort zone. Fear seems to be the monster behind so many things that we never attempt to do or shut down immediately. What's the harm in saying yes?

The next time you hear a story about someone and you don't understand their actions or maybe the choices they made in life, try to keep an open mind. After all everyone has a story. You may not understand it but at the very least attempt to view it from a different perspective.

Chapter 15

Success and money...

One of my favorite songs by Drake is called "Successful." He discusses the things that he wants in life and says in the end he just wants to be successful. It's a great song. I'm always concerned about being successful. I desire success from my own standards as well as the people that matter to me the most. What exactly determines if you or I are successful? Is it the amount of money that we generate? Is it the amount of people that we influence? Is it giving back to our community?

I personally think success is a combination of strategies and influences. Many of us are on a mission of financial gain. I'm always curious to know if the financial gain quest is for the right reasons. Maybe I shouldn't say right reasons because what's right to me may not be the same for you. I desire financial wealth to eliminate debt, so I can take care of my parents when they are unable to take care of themselves. I would love for my nieces and future children to never know anything about student loans or any massive debt. I want them to be able to live at home until they have enough money saved in the bank for a great start in life after, they have completed college and are well within their careers. Hopefully they'll pass the tradition on to their children.

It often seems that people are more infatuated with material things that immediately decrease in value after the time of purchase. All the material items that you want can be obtained at anytime. I can name lots of material items that I've had at a time when I wasn't or at least when I didn't consider myself as successful. Material items shouldn't make or break you. You should make the items because you are wearing them. You're the prize. Part of being successful is implementing what you believe in. Striving for what you think best suit's you in life regardless if the odds are against you. Sometimes the odds aren't against us and we are just scared to try something different or what other people will think about our decisions.

Being successful can be as simple as taking care of your responsibilities in life. That can be maintaining your household, being the best parent you can be, or just being the best person you can be. Being the best person you can be is highly favored in my book. There is nothing worst than meeting someone that you admire or consider successful but they constantly miss out on being the best person they can be by having ugly behavior. Being successful is being able to sit in a room full of people with the same or more credentials and experience as you possess and not have a jealous feeling or a feeling of uncertainty. Do not think because you have money (whatever your definition of that may be) that you are automatically successful. Financial gain is a piece of the success aspect. There are numerous people that are rich drug addicts and child abusers: Child abusers as in neglectful. There are people with means that don't give back to their communities. Giving back and paying it forward are ultimate tests of success. If you are from a neighborhood where there are children living in poverty why wouldn't you want to help feed them or organize an event to feed them or help them in some way.

If you have a platform and you know someone that's working toward obtaining their own platform why wouldn't you connect them with the right people? You must be a believer in that person's work or field but, that is an example of paying it forward. No one gets anywhere without help from someone. Sometimes on our journey to success we forget about the inklings or massive shoves we received from different people along the way. It doesn't matter how small the gesture of help may have been. It helped you to get where you are today. Recognizing and acknowledging others is important to success. Success is being comfortable with your status, understanding and respecting the process of working towards your life goals, being the best human you can be, giving back, paying it forward, and acknowledging those that have helped you along the way.

Now ask yourself if you are working toward your goals. If you have finished your first set of goals set new ones. When you set new goals for yourself that means you are always improving. You're constantly challenging yourself. Do you acknowledge and appreciate the assistance you've received along the way? Paying it forward and giving back can be something as small as volunteering at a soup kitchen or at a nursing home. Becoming a Coach or mentor to someone is paying your current knowledge and experience forward. Now that you've heard my definitions of being successful are you a success?

Conclusion

Play to Win!

Most people reflect on some of their past actions in life which, is normal. Reflecting and dwelling are not the same concept. The younger version of you still lives within. You know that compartment in your mind where you think about the things you used to do? That's where the younger you is stored. If you could tell your younger self something what would you say? Do you think the younger version of you would be receptive to the advice? If you have younger siblings or relatives would you give them the same advice that you would give your younger self?

Everyone suffers through some form of hardships in life. Some people have to deal with multiple hardships concurrently. That's just an unpleasant part of life. You have to make the best choices that you can possibly make for yourself with all situations and challenges you are faced with. There is no Butterfly affect or Albert Einstein (anymore) therefore we can't change what has already happened. If you are holding on to any ill feelings about another person you're preventing yourself from living the best possible life that you can. Have you ever noticed that when life throws something at you that pushes you a step back you get upset and start thinking about things and people that you're pissed with that have nothing to do with the current situation? That's because you haven't freed yourself to forgive them and you haven't forgiven yourself for allowing someone else to have that much power over your mind and emotions.

How we react to those events ultimately determine the outcome. I can become very irate when I feel someone is trying to take advantage of me, or if I feel mistreated in anyway. I know that cursing and fussing isn't going to change anything and will probably make the situation worse. We all have our freak out moments from time to time, especially when we feel like we just can't deal with any more surprise disappointments, that's human nature. The less freak-outs that we have, the better off we'll be as well as our minds. You can't think clearly when you're over reacting. . In fact overreacting almost always makes things worse. We have to think then react.

There are people living with terminal illnesses that are in better spirits than healthy human beings walking the Earth. I had a client literally on his death-bed making jokes and just seemed zealous over all. This past year one of my life mentor's Annette Perry lost her battle to cancer. I had never seen her complain about her pain until the very end. If she could remain in good spirits so can you. Then I hear people walking around complaining and actually sad as if their world is coming to an end because their significant other dumped them or just because they want to be in a relationship. Some people are suicidal about money. Do you see how minimal these issues are compared to a person with a terminal illness?

Remember to keep some things to yourself. You may have a great idea and want to share it with others. I know that feeling all too well. However, some of the best planned, projects or adventures are the ones you keep to yourself. Write them down and create a plan after all it would be a tragedy for someone else to use your idea and claim it as their own. Everything is not for everyone to know. Maintain some sort of privacy.

How to Play the Game of Life

We all strive to be better in life. We all desire more than what we currently have. Remember there is always someone that has a worse situation than you. Be appreciative for what you have and open to what you can create for yourself!

You are amazing, you are special, and you are enough!

Workbook!

**LIST 5 TO 10 AREAS OF YOUR LIFE OR YOUR PER-
SONALITY THAT YOU WOULD LIKE TO CHANGE.**

1.

2.

3.

4.

5.

6.

7.

8.

9.

10.

LIST 10 POSITIVE STEPS YOU CAN PERFORM TO ACHIEVE THE CHANGES LISTED ABOVE.

1.

2.

3.

4.

5.

6.

7.

8.

9.

10.

"When life gives you lemons,

make lemon drops!"

LetsTalkRaeStyle.com

Visit www.LetsTalkRaeStyle.com to view more literature by Ashley Rae.

www.ingramcontent.com/pod-product-compliance
Lightning Source LLC
Chambersburg PA
CBHW051836040426
42447CB00006B/556